Copyright © 2016 Inspired to Grace

Scripture quotations are from the following:

Scripture taken from the Holy Bible, NEW INTERNATIONAL VERSION®, NIV® Copyright © 1973, 1978, 1984, 2011 by Biblica, Inc.® Used by permission. All rights reserved worldwide. NEW INTERNATIONAL VERSION® and NIV® are registered trademarks of Biblica, Inc. Use of either trademark for the offering of goods or services requires the prior written consent of Biblica US, Inc.

Revised Standard Version of the Bible, copyright 1952 [2nd edition, 1971] by the Division of Christian Education of the National Council of the Churches of Christ in the United States of America. Used by permission. All rights reserved.

Scripture quotations marked HCSB®, are taken from the Holman Christian Standard Bible®, Copyright © 1999, 2000, 2002, 2003, 2009 by Holman Bible Publishers. Used by permission. HCSB® is a federally registered trademark of Holman Bible Publishers.

Scripture taken from the New King James Version. Copyright © 1982 by Thomas Nelson, Inc. Used by permission. All rights reserved.

The Holy Bible, King James Version. Cambridge Edition: 1769. Public Domain.

Scripture texts in this work are taken from the New American Bible, revised edition © 2010, 1991, 1986, 1970 Confraternity of Christian Doctrine, Washington, D.C. and are used by permission of the copyright owner. All Rights Reserved. No part of the New American Bible may be reproduced in any form without permission in writing from the copyright owner.

All rights reserved.

ISBN-13: 978-1945888472
ISBN-10: 1945888474

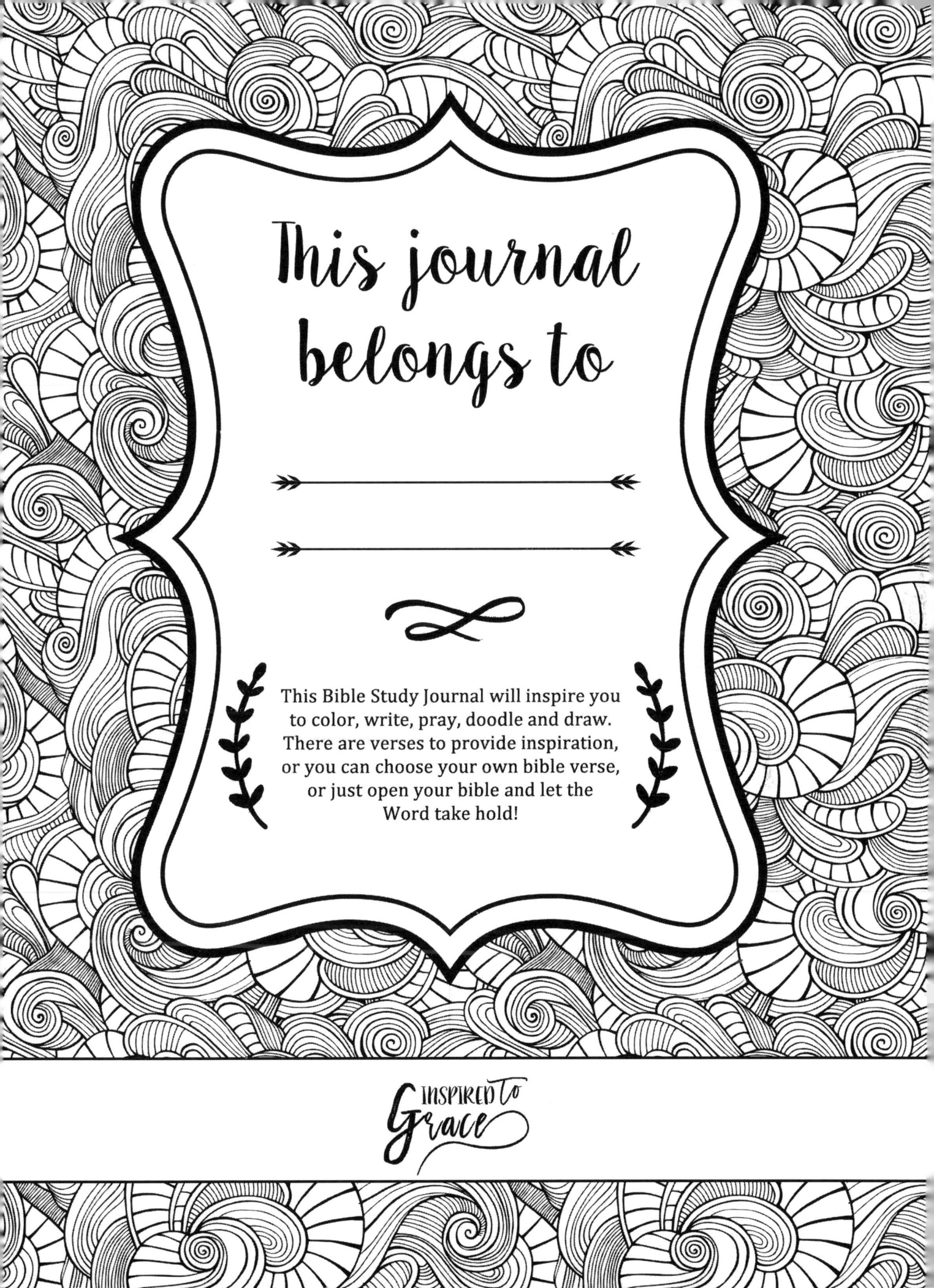

FREEBIES!

FREE PRINT DOWNLOADS

www.inspiredtograce.com/itgstudy

YOUR DOWNLOAD CODE : BSJ7833

 @inspiredtograce

 Inspired to Grace

Today's date:

Scripture:

Reflections:

Prayers:

Today's date:

Scripture:

Reflections:

Prayers:

Today's date:

Scripture:

Reflections:

Prayers:

Today's date:

Scripture:

Reflections:

Prayers:

Today's date:

Scripture:

Reflections:

Prayers:

Today's date:

Scripture:

Reflections:

Prayers:

Today's date:

Scripture:

Reflections:

Prayers:

Today's date:

Scripture:

Reflections:

Prayers:

Today's date:

Scripture:

Reflections:

Prayers:

Today's date:

Scripture:

Reflections:

Prayers:

Today's date:

Scripture:

Reflections:

Prayers:

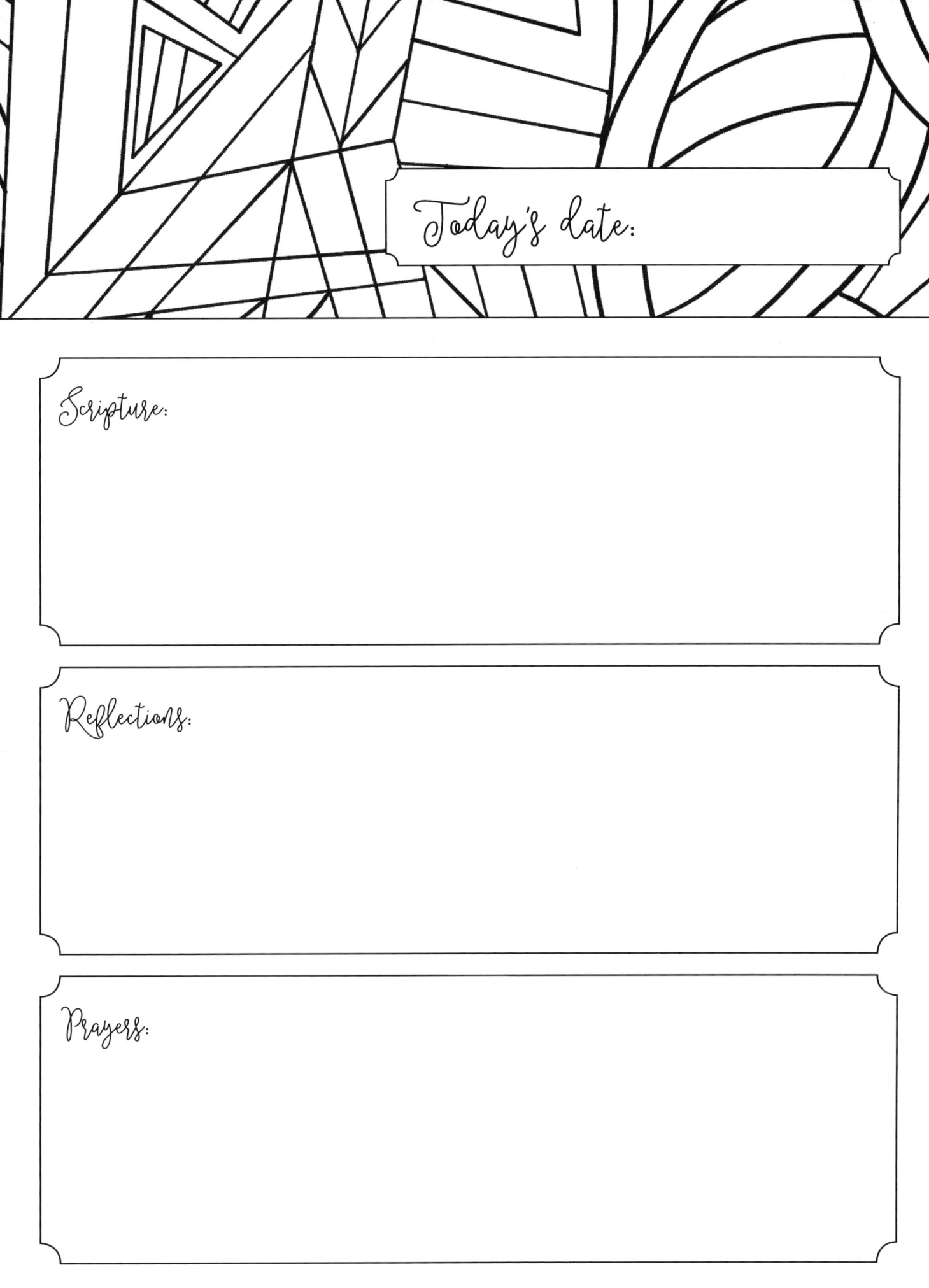

Today's date:

Scripture:

Reflections:

Prayers:

Today's date:

Scripture:

Reflections:

Prayers:

Today's date:

Scripture:

Reflections:

Prayers:

Today's date:

Scripture:

Reflections:

Prayers:

Today's date:

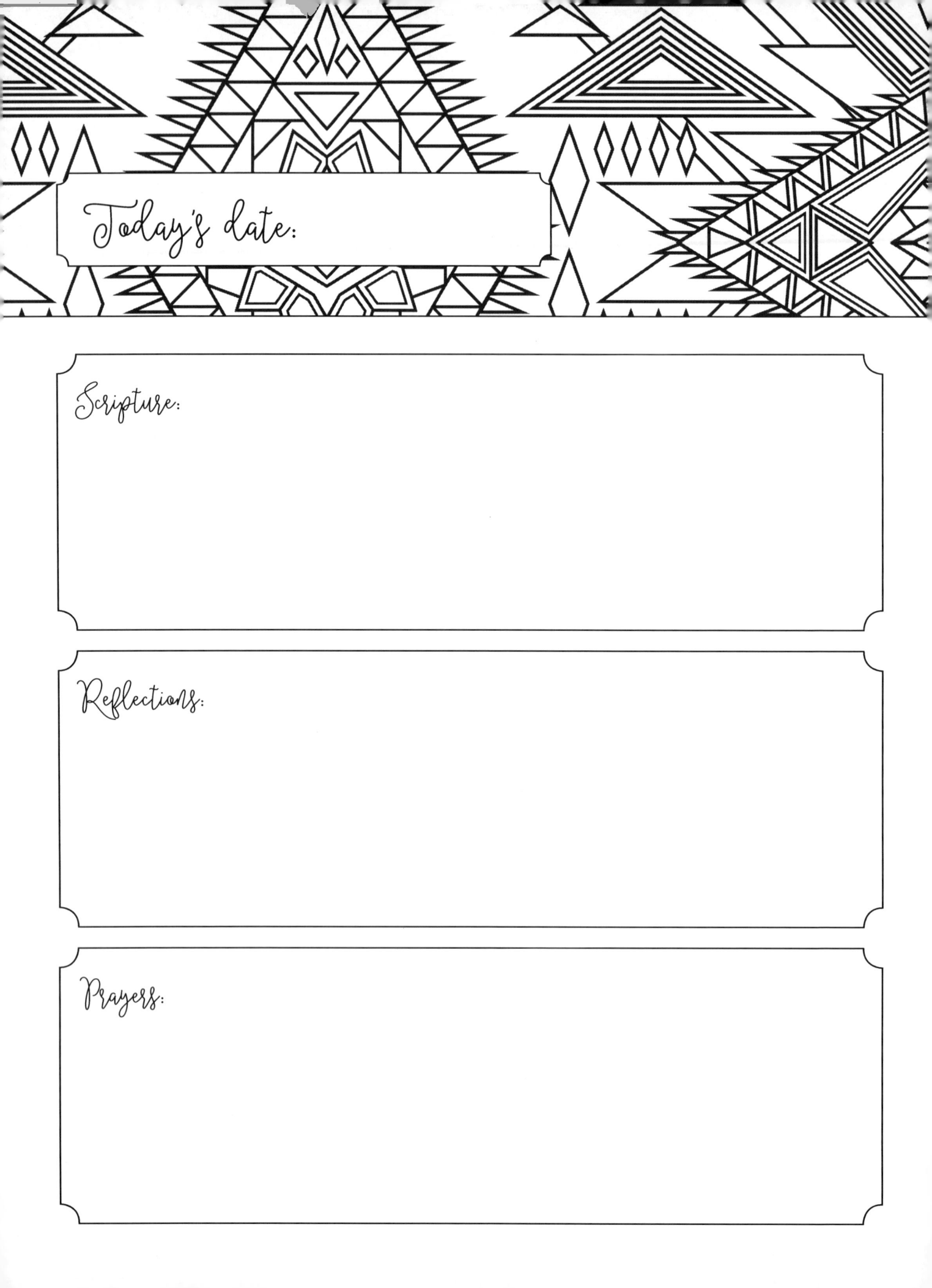

Scripture:

Reflections:

Prayers:

Today's date:

Scripture:

Reflections:

Prayers:

Today's date:

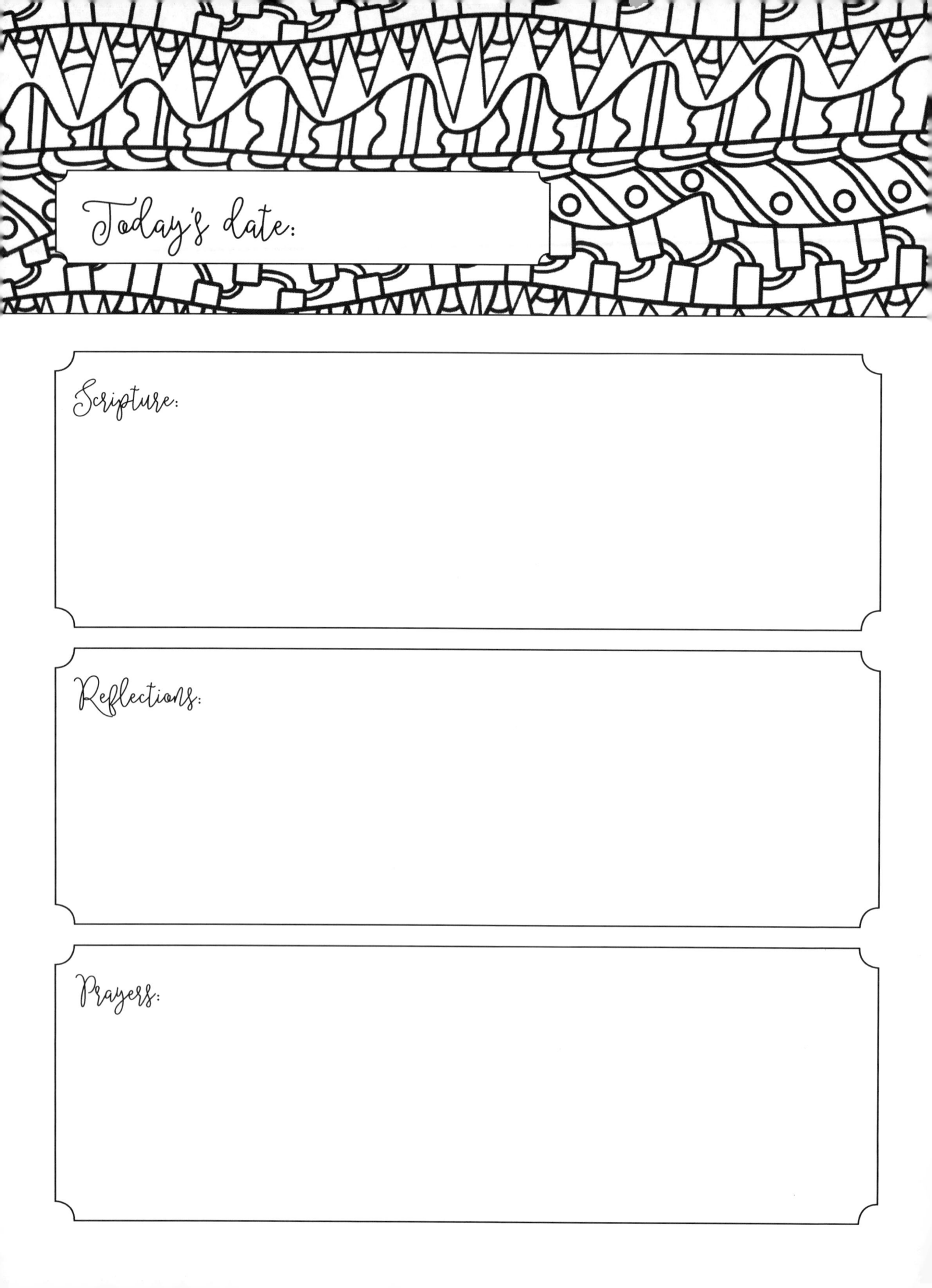

Scripture:

Reflections:

Prayers:

Today's date:

Scripture:

Reflections:

Prayers:

Today's date:

Scripture:

Reflections:

Prayers:

Today's date:

Scripture:

Reflections:

Prayers:

Today's date:

Scripture:

Reflections:

Prayers:

Today's date:

Scripture:

Reflections:

Prayers:

Today's date:

Scripture:

Reflections:

Prayers:

Today's date:

Scripture:

Reflections:

Prayers:

Today's date:

Scripture:

Reflections:

Prayers:

Today's date:

Scripture:

Reflections:

Prayers:

Today's date:

Scripture:

Reflections:

Prayers:

Today's date:

Scripture:

Reflections:

Prayers:

Today's date:

Scripture:

Reflections:

Prayers:

Today's date:

Scripture:

Reflections:

Prayers:

Today's date:

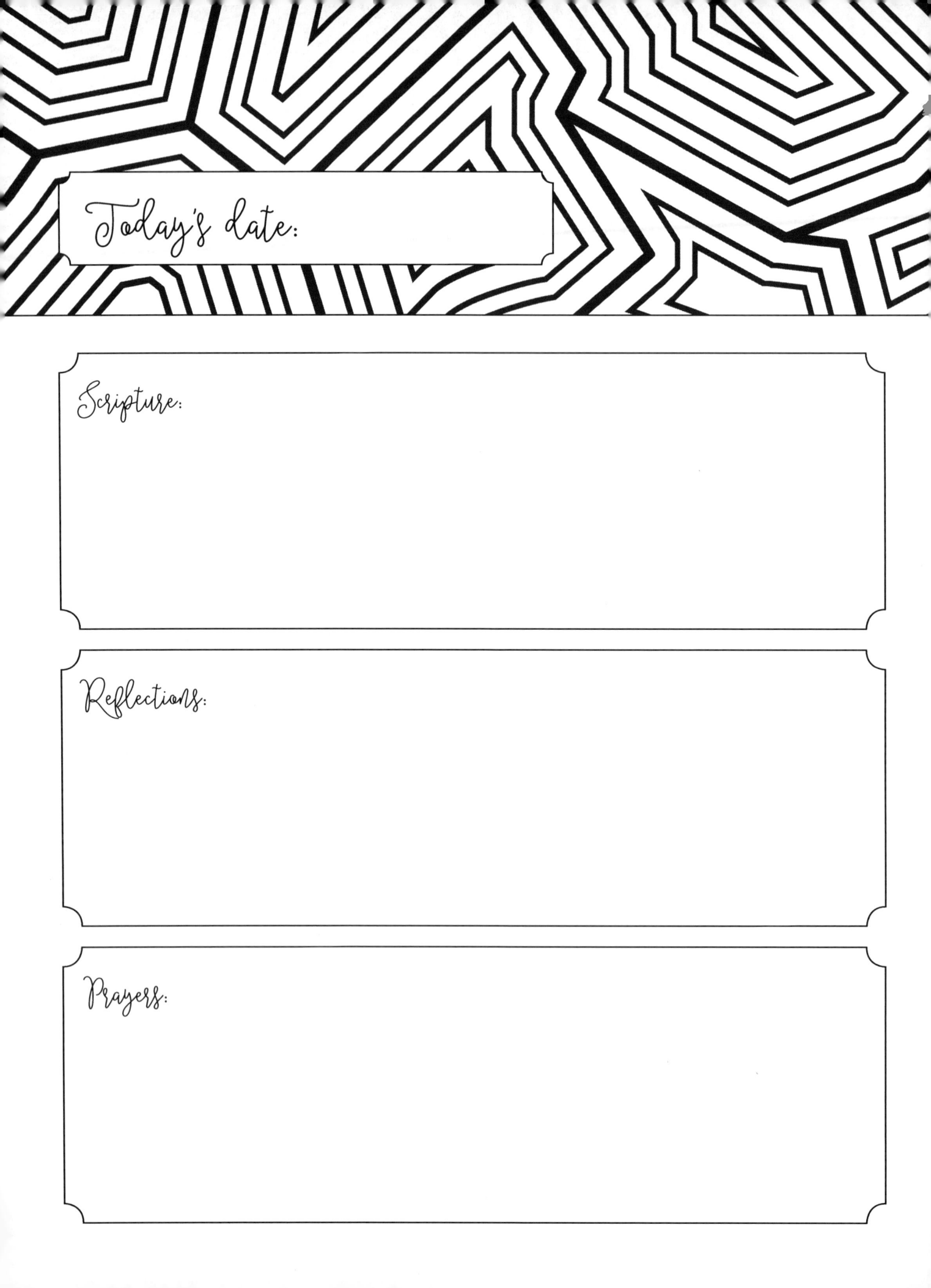

Scripture:

Reflections:

Prayers:

Today's date:

Scripture:

Reflections:

Prayers:

Today's date:

Scripture:

Reflections:

Prayers:

Today's date:

Scripture:

Reflections:

Prayers:

Today's date:

Scripture:

Reflections:

Prayers:

Today's date:

Scripture:

Reflections:

Prayers:

Today's date:

Scripture:

Reflections:

Prayers:

Today's date:

Scripture:

Reflections:

Prayers:

Today's date:

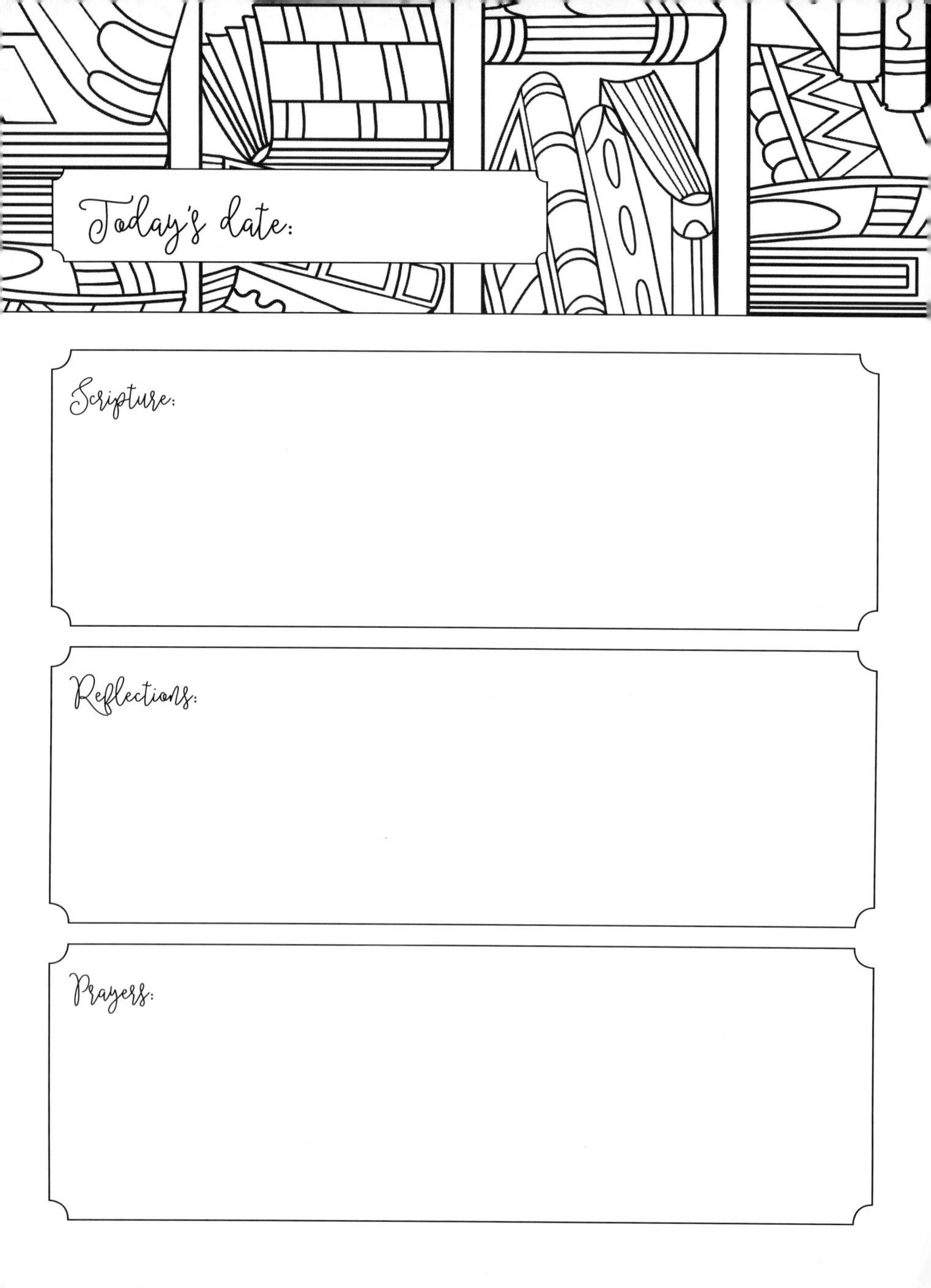

Scripture:

Reflections:

Prayers:

Today's date:

Scripture:

Reflections:

Prayers:

Today's date:

Scripture:

Reflections:

Prayers:

Today's date:

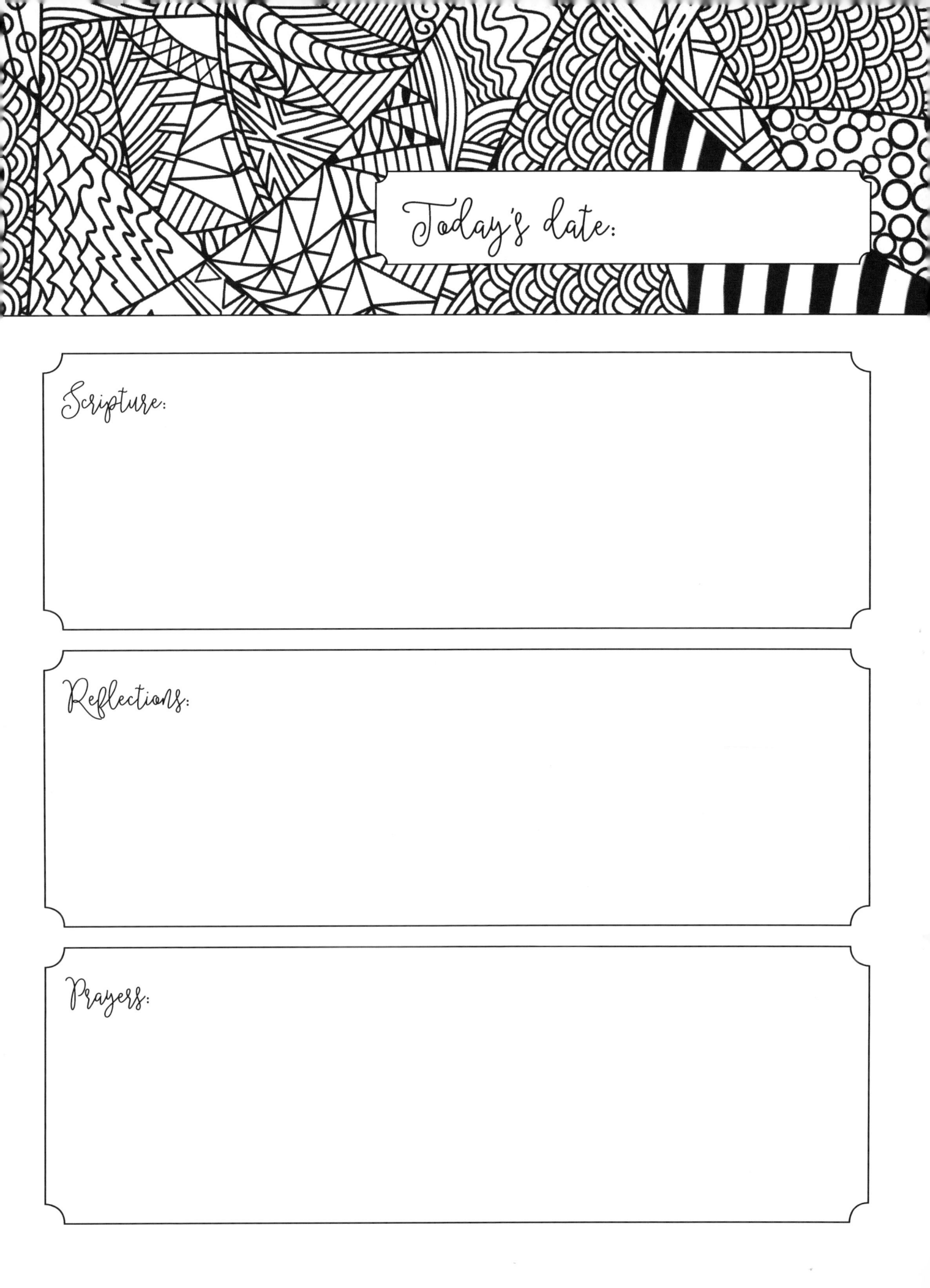

Scripture:

Reflections:

Prayers:

Today's date:

Scripture:

Reflections:

Prayers:

Today's date:

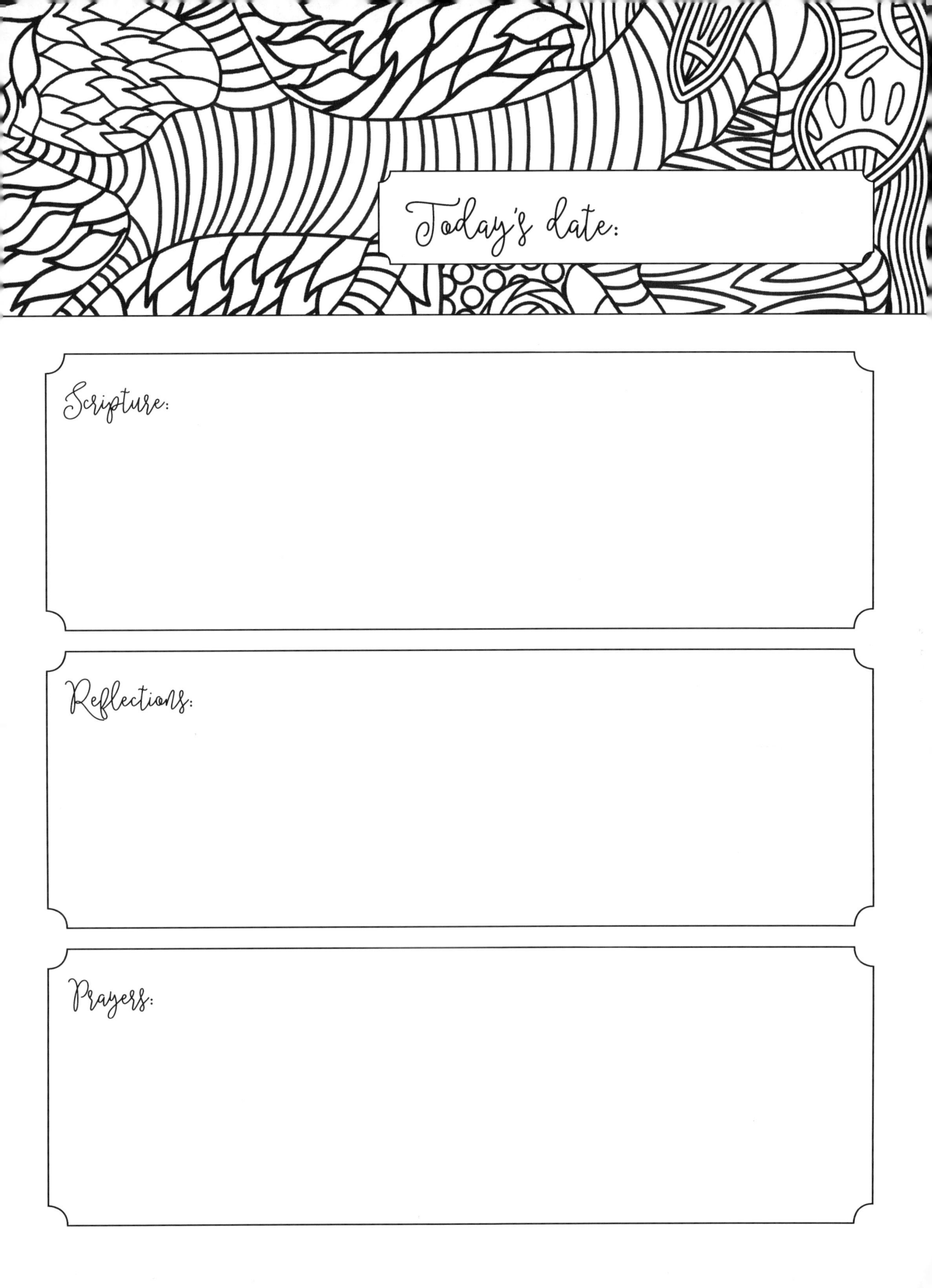

Scripture:

Reflections:

Prayers:

Today's date:

Scripture:

Reflections:

Prayers:

Today's date:

Scripture:

Reflections:

Prayers:

Today's date:

Scripture:

Reflections:

Prayers:

Today's date:

Scripture:

Reflections:

Prayers:

Today's date:

Scripture:

Reflections:

Prayers:

Today's date:

Scripture:

Reflections:

Prayers:

Today's date:

Scripture:

Reflections:

Prayers:

Today's date:

Scripture:

Reflections:

Prayers:

Today's date:

Scripture:

Reflections:

Prayers:

Today's date:

Scripture:

Reflections:

Prayers:

Today's date:

Scripture:

Reflections:

Prayers:

Today's date:

Scripture:

Reflections:

Prayers:

Today's date:

Scripture:

Reflections:

Prayers:

Today's date:

Scripture:

Reflections:

Prayers:

Today's date:

Scripture:

Reflections:

Prayers:

Today's date:

Scripture:

Reflections:

Prayers:

Today's date:

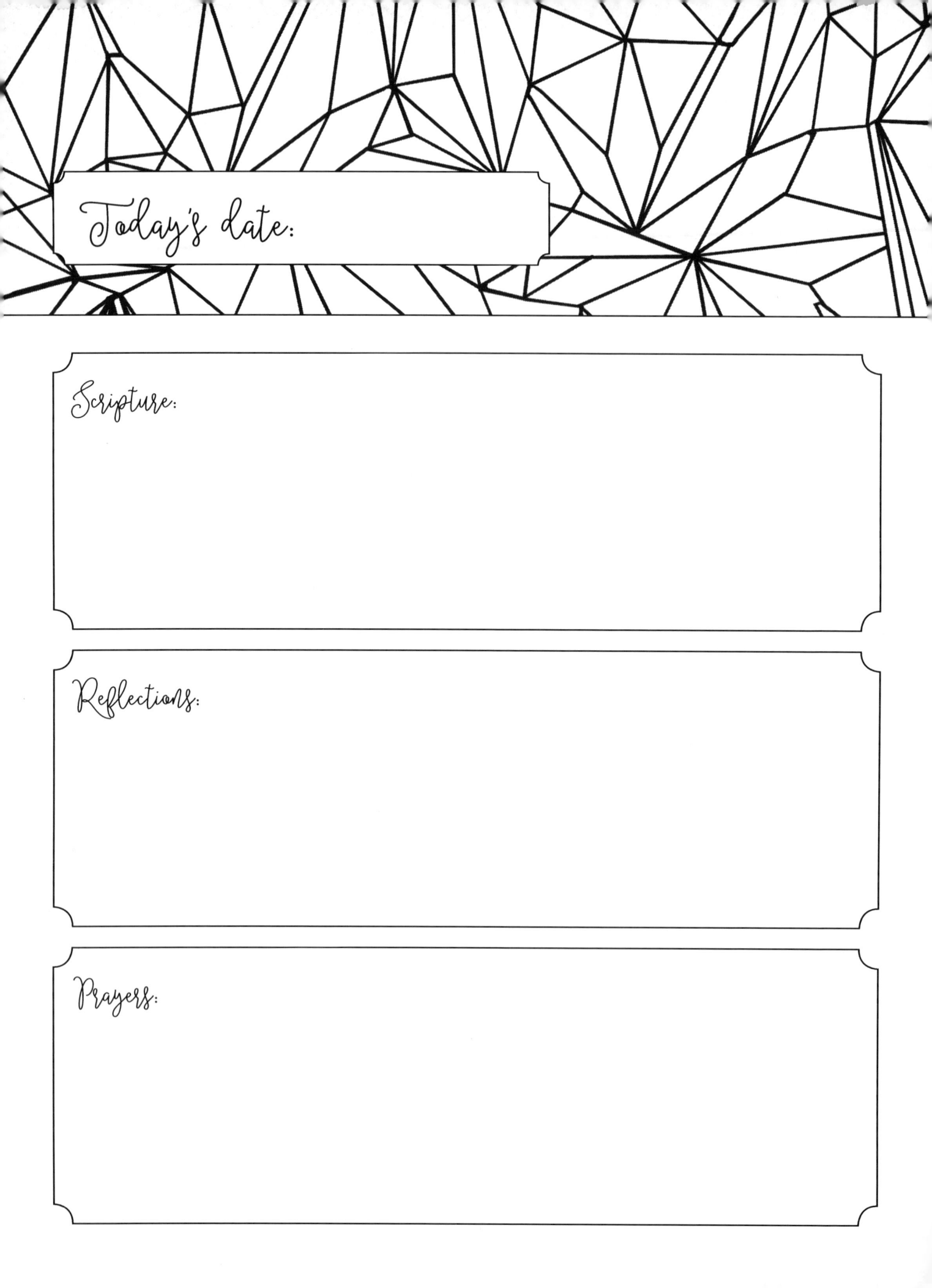

Scripture:

Reflections:

Prayers:

Today's date:

Scripture:

Reflections:

Prayers:

Today's date:

Scripture:

Reflections:

Prayers:

Today's date:

Scripture:

Reflections:

Prayers:

Today's date:

Scripture:

Reflections:

Prayers:

Today's date:

Scripture:

Reflections:

Prayers:

Today's date:

Scripture:

Reflections:

Prayers:

Today's date:

Scripture:

Reflections:

Prayers:

Today's date:

Scripture:

Reflections:

Prayers:

Today's date:

Scripture:

Reflections:

Prayers:

Today's date:

Scripture:

Reflections:

Prayers:

Today's date:

Scripture:

Reflections:

Prayers:

Today's date:

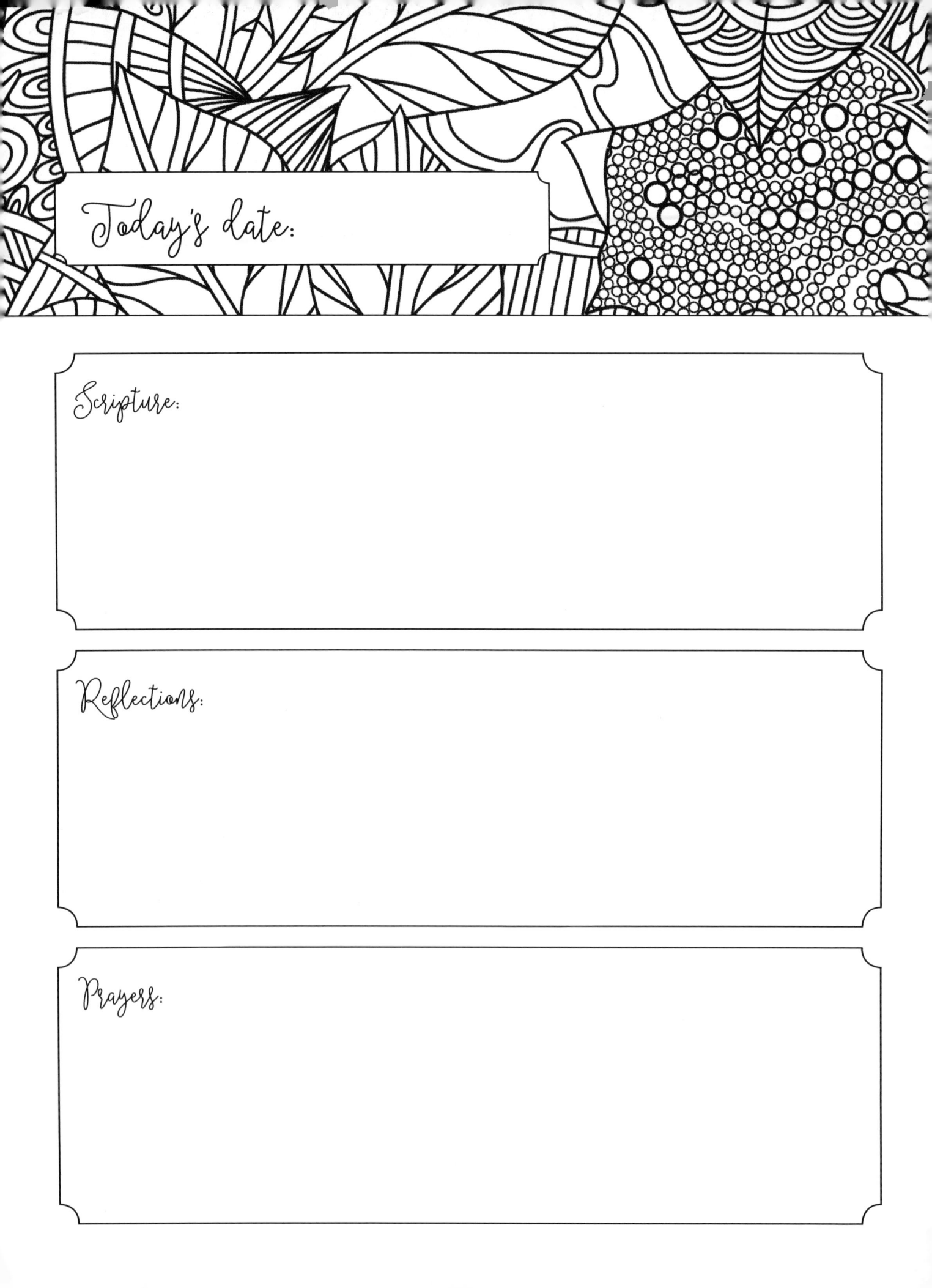

Scripture:

Reflections:

Prayers:

Today's date:

Scripture:

Reflections:

Prayers:

Today's date:

Scripture:

Reflections:

Prayers:

Today's date:

Scripture:

Reflections:

Prayers:

Today's date:

Scripture:

Reflections:

Prayers:

Today's date:

Scripture:

Reflections:

Prayers:

Today's date:

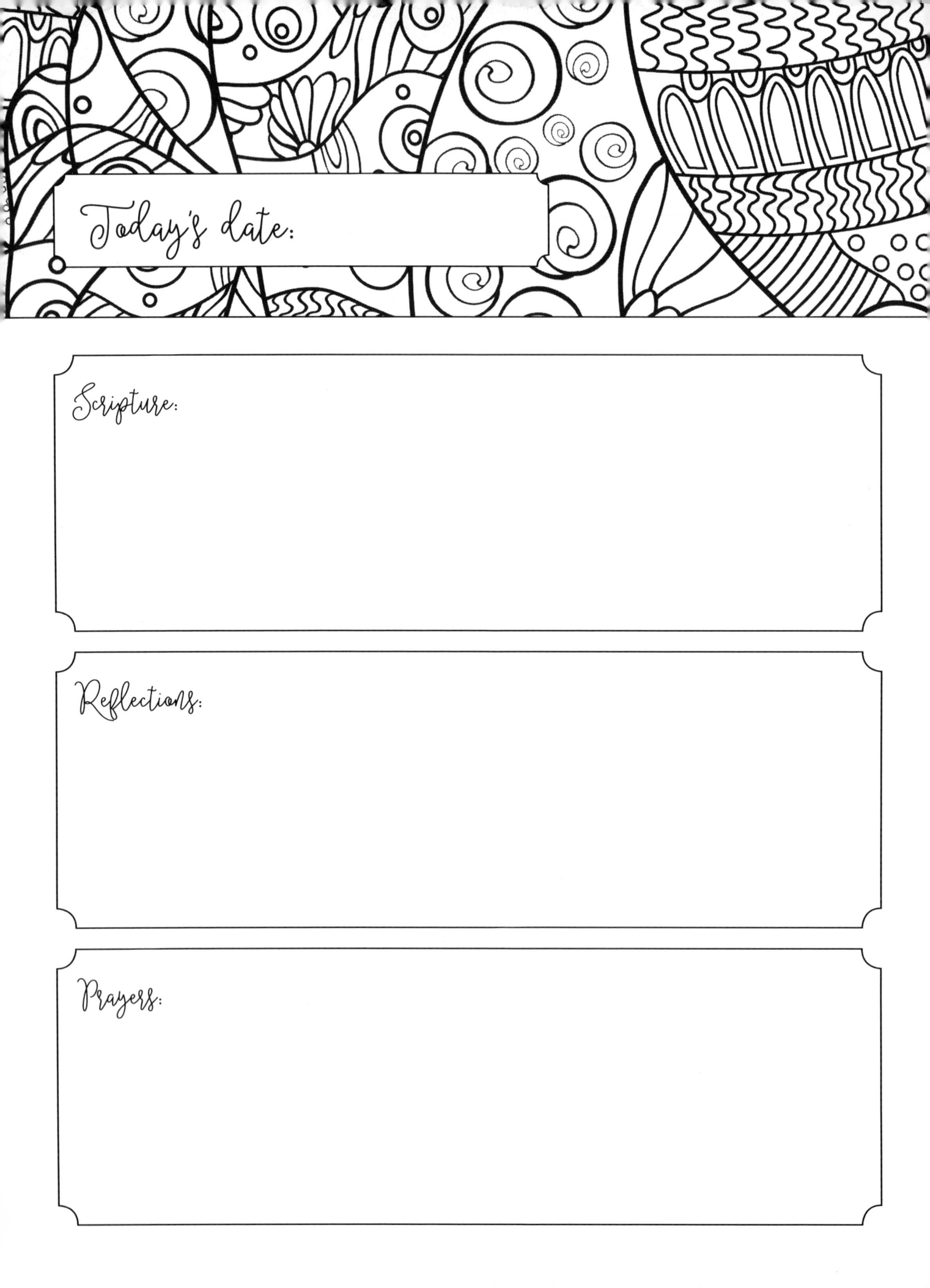

Scripture:

Reflections:

Prayers:

Today's date:

Scripture:

Reflections:

Prayers:

Today's date:

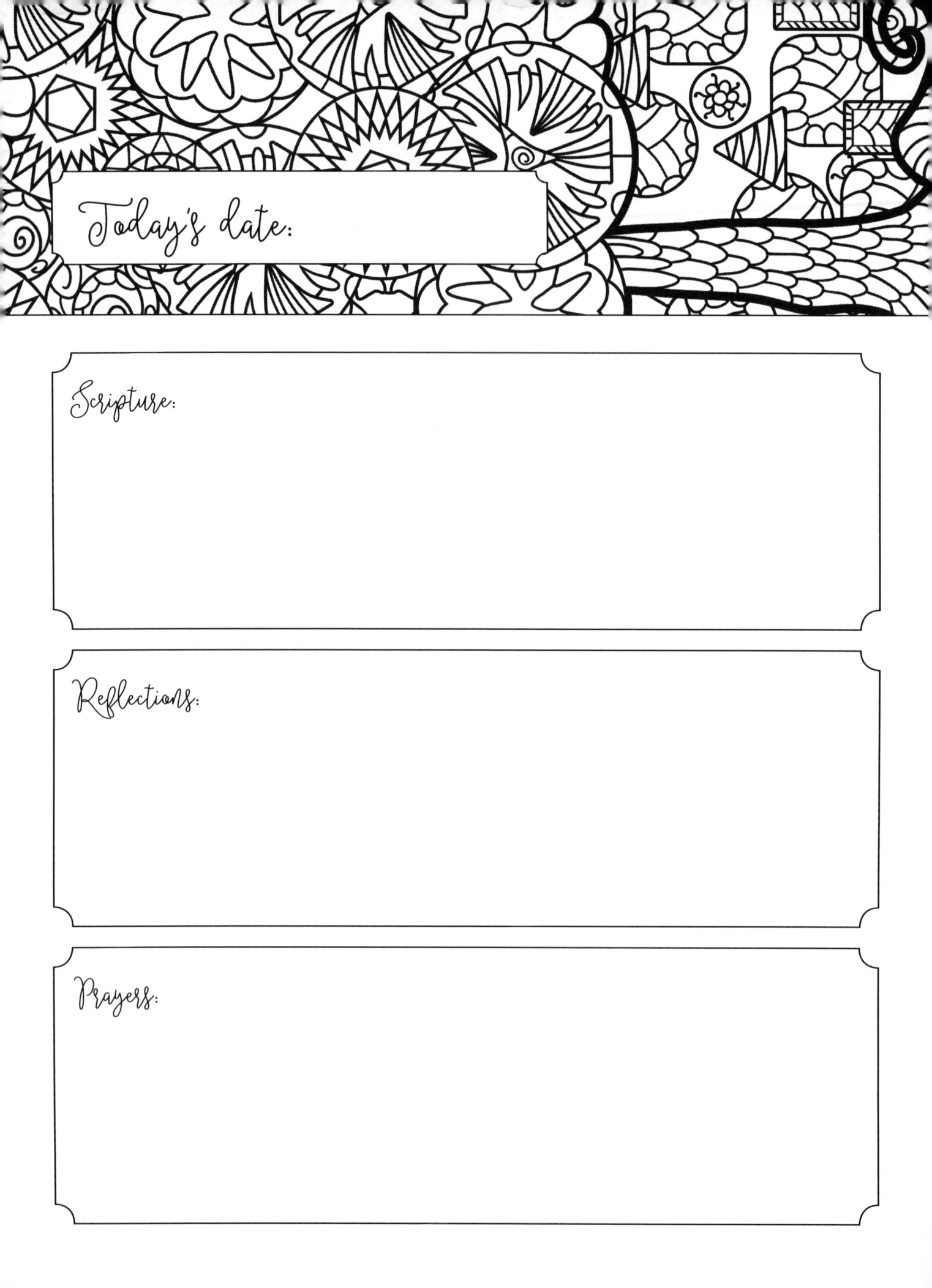

Scripture:

Reflections:

Prayers:

Today's date:

Scripture:

Reflections:

Prayers:

Today's date:

Scripture:

Reflections:

Prayers:

Today's date:

Scripture:

Reflections:

Prayers:

Today's date:

Scripture:

Reflections:

Prayers:

Today's date:

Scripture:

Reflections:

Prayers:

Today's date:

Scripture:

Reflections:

Prayers:

FREEBIES!

FREE PRINT DOWNLOADS
www.inspiredtograce.com/itgstudy

YOUR DOWNLOAD CODE: BSJ7833

@inspiredtograce

Inspired to Grace